Introduction:

Thank you for picking up this book. What is Marketing
With a Soul? Its about taking the chances of being your own
boss no matter if it is being in the service industry like
massage therapy, chiropractor, Reiki Practitioner, or in
network or multi-level marketing. Its about how do you
market yourself, and not loose sight of what it is that you
wanted to do, and to completely, as best you can, come from
a heart felt and open space. Its about letting things come in,
and be successful and be able to sleep at night.

I remember when I was a marketing major for not
even one semester in college. One of my professors started
classes with I am gonna teach you how to get people to buy,
what they don't need, and sleep at night. That notion chilled
me to the bone and still does.

For the longest time I thought that was just him, but I

will stay away from all that. I then found a network marketing company that I wanted to work and do really well with. I attended trainings, read books on marketing, and taught how to grow downlines and get paid really well for it. It was when my upline looked at me and we were trying to figure out how much our time was worth and that even personal time has dollar signs on it. That made me want to jump out in traffic. It was then and there I never again, wanted to be that person. I hope that this book helps many not become so lost in the business they can not enjoy their success.

Chapter 1: The Color of a Mission

What is a mission. Its about what you wanna do. That is the reason you have to accept them. What is the passion behind what you are either about to endeavor upon or have done for years? I have worked in network marketing as well as marketing myself as an intuitive reader and motivational speaker.

I have seen time and time again myself and others fail in the area of marketing due to them never realizing what their true passion for what they were doing was, or they lost sight of it. This first lesson is about teaching you how to rediscover what the passion in your work is, and make sure that it echoes what it is that you are trying to portray.

With any business there is a business model. When you begin any business the first thing that anyone will tell you to do is to create a mission statement. This mission statement, if a business wants to do well will be what each action, program, each initiative will follow and entail. This means that anytime your company does this, you should be able to take your finger on any line of writing produced by the company, and it should fall into the mission statement.

Now, I am not going to be instructing you on the mission statement of your business, we are going to be talking about the thing that dictates everything. Your life's mission statement. What do you stand for? What is it that each and every aspect of your life reflects? When you are network marketing, marketing for massage therapy, acupuncture, Reiki, or retail business, etc one has to make sure that the life of the business owner is as balanced as possible, or the business shall be a reflection of that.

Firstly take a moment to think about your life. What

are your beliefs? What do you stand for? How do you want to portray yourself? Write a small paragraph (3-8 sentences in length), that describes your life's mission statement. I will share mine to give you an example but feel free to develop your own as this is your life's mission statement. There are no wrong choices in your life.

I want to wake up each morning, happy with all the deeds I have been apart of the day before. I want to honor my ancestors, my beliefs and strive no matter what to see God in each person that I interact with. I wish to spread joy and peace, and each day be blessed to watch a face light up when they come to a realization of a deeper truth for them. I will be open to all people no matter what their back story, I promise to meet them in the space that I interact with them, and allow the divine energy that dwells in me to be shown in all I do. I will love.

Write down your own life's mission statement. You will keep this in safe place. Frame it, keep it somewhere that means to you, and that you will see it everyday. The more you remind yourself of what you stand for, the easier it is to keep tack of if you are fulfilling it.

Ok, so now that you have your life's mission statement what can you do with that, and what does it have to do with the business? If life is not in order then business will fall apart they can not be out of sync. Your life's mission statement cannot be more important than any individual part of your being. Now what you must do is ask your self why you want to do these things. We as human beings work on the reward system. What am I going to get out of that? I know that sounds a little cold, and spoiled. However, when we ask ourselves why we want something it gets us closer to our authentic self, our true self, our true life's mission.

How do you do that? Well let 痴 take my mission statement and I will show you the process in which I go through when I am trying to decide what it is that I want. My first sentence in my mission statement is: *I want to wake up each morning, happy with all the deeds I have been apart of the day before.*

Ok so why? Why would I care what I did before, or why do I want my first thought in the morning to not be cofffeeeeeeeee!!!! My spiritual practices teach me that each action I make is a mark in my story that I wrote before I got here. When I wake up its important for me to be able to look in the mirror and know that no matter what happened the day before, I am OK with how I interacted and stood by my moral and ethical thoughts.

Now, once you have the mission statement completed, and you have asked yourself why you want to do the things that you are doing, you have the beginning of the the ability to keep and assure your passion in your marketing career. This will also allow you to keep perspective on your passion.

Fear not, life mission statements as well as business mission statements are the ideas that you hold while you write them. You can at any point when things change (perspectives, beliefs, thoughts and practices), the statement too can change.

Now that you know what you will stand for, you will now be finding out color identification of your traits. When marketing to people since marketing is all about creating relationships you should be able to know which color they are and you can market to them. This part is a deeper side of getting to know who you are.

Why are we spending so much time in getting to know our inner selves? As with everything in our lives, the better and stronger foundation that we have, the stronger you can grow as a person as well as a business. The philosophy of color personality identification is an old study that I have found very helpful both for myself, as well as identifying and helping the needs of my clients and customers.

The idea behind color personality is that you have a dominate color personality and when you identify that, it can tell you things about how you learn, and help you look for the imbalances within your mind body and soul.

Once you have discovered these things you can take even the "weaker" attributes of yourself, and turn them into things to help. For instance a blue personality has the need to be social and liked. Best job for them would be in network marketing as a leader, interacting with people, but perhaps an online business might not suit them.

It's not about judging your likes and dislikes, but about using them and understanding them to create the best business dynamic for you. Now read the following descriptions of each color and find the one that best describes you.

The Blue Personality: Analyzer/Organizer

A Blue personality uses its five physical senses to access information. As an emotionally driven personality, blue needs to be liked and accepted. It is one of the "needs" that can cause apprehension in your personality. Blue's will assist others, and want to be accepted by the whole group. They will be leaders when someone asks them to be. They possess highly developed powers of observation and a scientific intuition. Family is important and they sometimes find themselves in a caretaker role or of taking care of others.

Tendencies

The tendencies of Blue's are the desire for orderliness, conscientious, disciplined, precise, thorough, diplomatic with people, analytical, planned, and scheduled.

Green Personality: Helper/Supporter

A strong Green individual lives in a world of intangibles where hopes, dreams and emotions are most important. You look at the big picture, are not detail oriented, and like to explore possibilities and alternative ways of doing things.

You march to your own drummer and frequently find it difficult to get on the same wavelength as others. This often puts pressure on your relationships. You require a environment where you can be imaginative, and creative. Its all about being able to use your creativity to find solutions to problems rather than cold facts. Your intuition is highly developed and you seem to be able to sense what others are feeling.

Tendencies

The tendencies of Green's are being supportive, agreeable, loyal, a lot of self control, consistency, Good Listener, and have a natural ability to develop personal relationships quickly.

Red Personality: Leader/Promoter

A dominant Red score indicates life痴 experiences must make sense to you. You are logical, practical and do not display emotions easily. Because of your desire for structure, you seek control of both your environment and people, and are sometimes seen by others as domineering. You are punctual and may become irritated if you think your time is being wasted. Schedules, plans, blue prints, these are the most important tools in a Red's tool bx. As a natural leader, you are driven by the need for power and control. What stresses you is lack of organization and unexpected changes.

Tendencies

The tendencies of Red's are: getting immediate results, making quick decisions, persistent, solving problems, take charge, appearing completely self reliant, accepting challenges.

Yellow Personality: Creator/Performer

Yellows are self-confident personalities who will challenge anything and everything; authority, rules and established ways of thinking. This tendency to question everything can create a strained atmosphere in both business and personal situations. You are interested in theories, abstractions, innovations and change. You are a conceptual deep thinker and enjoy getting "lost in your head" as a way of exploring new ideas and looking for innovative ways to make a difference. You are a true "out-of-the-box" visionary and adept at mulch-tasking. Searching for the hidden meanings behind every day life gives you great pleasure.

Tendencies

The tendencies of Yellow's are very optimistic, a lot

of Enthusiasm, Make very good first impressions, verbally articulate, likes to help others, creates entertaining climate. Now we will look at things to grow and thrive both in business and the marketing world.

Blue:

Best Situation for these Colors

1. Being able to concentrate on detail

2. Opportunities to critique

3. Stable surroundings and procedures

4. Exact job description, expectations

5. Opportunities for "careful" planning

6. Sufficient time to do things right

7. Opportunities for reassurance from authority

Weaknesses

1. Indecisive (looking at all data)

2. Get bogged down in details

3. Rigid on the "how to's"

4. Avoids controversy

5. Low self esteem

6. Hesitant to try new things

7. Sensitive to criticism

8. Can be pessimistic

What they Need from Others

1. Quick decision making

2. Optimism

3. Help in persuading others

Growth Area

1. Be more open with their feelings

2. Be more optimistic

Green:

Best situation for them

1. Sincere appreciation by others

2. Minimal conflict between people

3. Security

4. Acknowledgment of work by others

5. Limited territory

6. Traditional procedures

7. Opportunity to develop personal relationships

Weaknesses

1. Resist change

2. Trouble making deadlines

3. Overly lenient with people

4. Procrastinates

5. Indecisive

6. Holds grudges

7. Overly possessive

8. Lacks initiative

Needs from Others

1. Push to try new challenges

2. Help in solving difficult problems

3. Initiative and accepting change

Growth area

1. Facing confrontation and dealing with it

2. Moving at a faster pace and initiating

Red:

Best situation for this color

1. New varied activities

2. Opportunity to really get things done

3. Continual challenges, mulch-tasker

4. Difficult assignments

5. Freedom to act from their instinct

6. Control over the situations

7. Direct answers from others, no innuendos

Weaknesses

1. Insensitivity towards others

2. Impatient

3. Overlook risks

4. Inflexibility, demanding of others

5. Talks too much

6. Inattentive to details at times

7. Resenting of restrictions

Need from Others

1. Attention to routine tasks

2. Caution

3. Focus on details and facts

Growth area

1. Greater patience

2. Sensitivity to others' needs

3. Flexibility

Yellow:

Best situation for These Colors

1. Friendly warm environment

2. Freedom from control

3. Public recognition of ability

4. Opportunity to talk

5. Positive reinforcement

6. Enthusiastic response to ideas

Weaknesses

1. Following through

2. Overestimating results

3. Misjudging capabilities

4. Talks too much

5. Acts impulsively

6. Jumps to conclusions

7. Over commits

8. Acts first, thinks second

Needs others to provide

1. Follow through on details

2. Focus on tasks

3. Logical approach

Growth area

1. Time awareness

2. Objectivity in decision making

Now that you have chosen your personality your color your assignment is to make a list of things in the marketing area that you can utilize your gifts in. How can you take both strength and weaknesses and grow your foundation and better your sense of self understanding.

Now that you have an understanding of the two most basic concepts in marketing and in basic business understanding you can take these skills and implement them into your personal life as well. There are times when I am dealing with family members in my head I have to remind my self, this person is a red, that is OK. This is how they

work. How can I help with what they need, so that we can

get this job done and all parties are taken care of.

Chapter 2: Being Welcomed

As we work on developing a marketing plan, the biggest thing to prepare is your follow up plan. Many people fail at this for two reasons. They don稚 do it at all, or they don稚 deliver things that apply to the person you are trying to market too.

The simplest thing that people do not do when trying to grow, or sustain their business is they do not follow up their clients. They will make phone calls and if they do not get an immediate response, they say they must not have been interested. They meet someone at a party and they get their information and send an email or leave a voice mail and leave it at that.

Now it is not about pestering the person to death. This happens a lot as well, and that will be discussed in Chapter 5 Keep your Friends and Family, however do not harass people. There is a difference in having a good solid follow up plan, and being called in for questioning.

Sales follow-up is one of the most common and important types of follow-up situations. These are the ones that are generated from leads. Either leads that were given to you, or someone actually approaching you for more information about your company. This type of follow-up positions you away from the competition so you can generate more business from your existing customers. It shows that your company has its act together and really cares about satisfying customers.

Follow-up isn't just about selling. It's about building relationships and allowing them to get to know you, the company, as well as eventually getting them to be apart of your business. This can be for your down line, or to have them come in for a cup of coffee to your cafe. This is important because each time a person interacts with you and or your business the feeling they leave with is the one that they will remember. If you do not follow up in a timely manner the person will think that they do not matter to you and will take their business elsewhere. If you over call, over email then they will feel desperation.

The reason that people fail at this is for the same reason. Self Esteem. If your self worth is not high then you will do one of two things. Start a million projects hoping that one of them will come to fruition. The other is to avoid following up and leave the ball in their court. Doing either of these things will destroy you and your business.

When working with your self-esteem you have to remember you are your business. Each and every day figure out a way that you can do things that make you feel good about your business. In spare time clean your office, and have a good organizing system. The more organized you are, the easier it is to find and do things. This is a sign of a clean and proper mind and heart, which will spill over into your business.

Another way to raise your self esteem is to journal each day and write out reasons why you are three W's of self esteem. Worthy, Wholesome, and Welcomed in the business word. Write things that support you. An example of this is as follows:

I am worthy of business as what I offer is a value to me. I am wholesome in all of my practices and people welcome me to be apart of their team.

Do company research. If possible do research on the person you are going to call back and see if you can figure out what color personality either the business is, or the person directly that you are going to call back.

You can do this with reading the companies mission

statement, and the type of business they are in. If you are in network marketing and you are dealing with individual people to join your team then reading them and figuring out what color personality is, once you have that you can cater your follow up with questions and conversation that relates to their color.

If the person is say a blue personality then you will be able to discuss how your products and or services will allow you to be more organized and focused. Say it痴 a food/supplement you can discuss how healthier people are more apt to be productive at work, and their bottom line is increased. Etc and so on.

Now, with that in mind there is a statement that I have heard in a lot of marketing and this applies mostly to the network marketing people. I had a lupine person tell me once, its not about being that customers best friend, its just about getting the sale, or its just about getting them to sign up. WRONG! Now you do not want very member of your team, or even all of your customers to be your best friends, however you do want to be able to have a conversation with them. If you have people who are so completely different, since business is about building a relationship there will be nothing to build on.

Now this can be cleared up by defining what a relationship is and what a friendship is. Webster's defines a relationship as: the way in which two or more concepts, objects, or people are connected, or the state of being connected. They define friendship as the emotions or conduct of friends; the state of being friends. Now this can help create the barrier between them all. You can have relationships with people, discussing the commonalities.

Friendships involve emotions. Emotions run the

whole gambit. A friend is someone who has to deal with your different opinions, a relationship does not. So its best to join in relationships that best suit you. If you are a pagan befriend a christian. If you are a mystical shop don't create a relationship with the people picketing out front. Not saying you cant befriend them. This also proves that friendships can also grow into relationships.

Actually that is the ideal and dream world, and if this is your goal to turn relationships into friendships, get a highlighter and be ready for chapter 5.

Your assignment in this section is to write three questions that a person will ask when you are following up with them, and then write your response based on the different color personalities and entice them.

Chapter 3: THE INTERNET

We have all been using online marketing in which to advertise and grow our business. Some of you even found this course on a social media or other online marketing tool. The thing as with all things they can become over saturated and with online tools it's very easy to start to ignore the input of information.

The thing to do, as with all marketing ideas, is to stand out. The problem is that we have gotten to the point as with all media, to go to an extreme. We have been this way for a few years. The good thing about this is people are already sick of this. They have been burnt out on the over stimulation that comes from media.

When doing online marketing you have to remember three things: Personal, Remembrance, and Returning. When you are looking at clients in the online sense you have to remember that it's even harder for them to get the personal experience if you do not follow the following easy steps.

1. Personal: Each person that comes into your frame of consciousness online needs to have that feeling of personal nature. Business is less about products that you have to offer, but the experience they have when they are going through it.

2. Remembrance. You have to stand out. Out of 10 businessman's that market about 5 of them fully or marginally suffice making things personal. However, when it comes to remembrance the impression that is left with the person is has to be fully positive. The old saying by Ms. Maya Angelou "People will never forget how you made them feel." This trumps all other impressions.

3. Returning: In marketing they will tell you that it does not matter if a person comes to you once. Each time

they need a service you provide they must come back to you. The other two pieces will make sure that this happens.

Each experience is one of the most over looked manners of marketing when focusing online. This is why a lot of marketing online does not work. We have broken down the two most popular ways to online market and will be sharing with you how to make each one of these a way to give a positive an uplifting experience.

Let's start with Face book. When you use Face book there are many things that you can do. You can create an ad, a page and a group. I tell people to do all three. Here is the difference to help you clear up things. An ad on Face book is something that you pay per click for. You run it and it's a picture with a quick description of your company. This is more for someone who has a big budget for marketing and can help bring people to either your website and or your page.

A face book page is a free tool where you can have people that are not your direct friends will be able to like your page. When a person likes your page your posts on this page will be able to be seen by these people. The greatest advantage of having a face book page is that you the name you put on this page, is what shows up in that way. It will look like your company is posting. So mine being called Pure Path when I post on this page, every time I or one of the people that works for me posts on the page it looks like the company is posting it.

A group is a great way to start conversations and creates a place where you can talk about subjects that relate to your products and services. This will allow you to not only to share your info, but to also with others posting about the subject you are most interested, and learn what others are doing in order to learn what to do, and also what not to do.

Twitter is one that I struggled with for a long time. However now that I fully understand its uses it works very well. The thing to do is only post about your business three times a day. Adding people that are not related to your companies services is very important. Cross marketing in all areas, other business owners, not just in your area. There are so many ways and being open and helping another business by re-tweeting their tweets makes you look more personal able and will help you in the long run.

Now, go out there and create a Face book page, a group, and if not already a personal page. The best way I have seen to use this, is use your personal page for that. Whats going on with you. You can talk about being excited, but try to keep business oriented posts on the business focused page.

The Face book group is a place where you can have people post things. Say if your business is about wellness, allow others to post things on a group. Post things to talk about that your products or services take care of. This is a get interest group. Its a way of starting leads, and beginning the process of not really over doing information for your your perspective clients.

Now after that, create a Face book page. This is all about business. Specials, compensation plans, reasons why they should choose you, or your products for what it is. Keep it simple. When it comes to advertising on Face book, do your research about your product or service and how has it hindered or enhanced people who do the same thing. You can Google questions simply as: "How has Face book advertising assisted people in X."This is the best way to do research and make sure for you, that advertising in this way will actually be beneficial.

Its about working what works, and also allowing to meet people where they are at. Not about forcing things done.

Chapter 4: The Egomania

We have all been there, and weather its graduating

from a service industry training, or you have found the absolute best product for you and you wanna go and be a missionary for the sham wow. The issue is that sometimes, out of the best of intentions we get a little bit of egomania. I have been there. When I joined Young Living, almost 11 years ago, I was like yup. This is it, there will be nothing else. Not only am I going to make sure that every person hears the good news of my product, and they too will then understand how they need this.

The issue is, how do you feel when door to door salesmen come to your door. Exactly. They are not bad people, they are just known for what they do. When we get touched by the spirit of direct sales, or service industry we to become a walking, 24 hour a day door to door salesperson. This is not a bad thing. We just have to learn to manage it, as well as avoid the ego mania so that we don't get lost in our message, and also to stop us from only becoming our message.

Much like a religious zealot, sometimes we can become the owner, founder, of enlightenment. Without this product or this service you can not live a happy life, or you will be forever sick etc.

The thing we have to remember is that this service, this product worked for you. It will work for others, however I have seen time and time again that people get so wrapped up in their product that when someone says no, and may legitimately not need this service or product, you take it as a personal attack and that is because, you have personalized the thing that you are in business with, as the only thing that is you.

We have to remember, you lived many years without this product or service. It was the right time for YOU, to find this thing, and it worked for YOU. You are not a alien, and its not just for you, however its not for everyone. You have to be OK with this fact.

The reason that you can have a business that you choose, and for the most part you are reading this book because you have made this decision to be your own boss, because we live in a free enterprise society. You can do this because you have the right to. Anyone can start a business. The ones that are successful, understand, support, and love that there are other businesses.

No matter what it is. You just have to drop the control and know in your heart that it works for you. When you come off as the only one that has the key. You have the new found cure. That its the only way, then you have come across as desperate, and in need of validation. Be the example much more than the Shepard.

Why is this important? Now that I have lectured you. This will be expounded upon in the next chapter, but its important that you realize. This worked for you. Its what you need. Otherwise you wouldn't have been involved. If you couldn't relate then you would have never picked it up. Take a holistic health service or product. If everyone around you is in pretty OK, and in shape, or they don't see the need for it, then no matter how much you talk to them, they will not resonate with it.

People love intrigue. They very rarely want things spelled out to them. They wanna have something catch their interest and then let them come to you. Asking "hey, you look, feel, or act different, whats up?" This is your ideal sales pitch. Where they have come to you, by seeing something, and then you can show them what you have done. It stays personal. Its not you saying you need to fix yourself, its this is what I have done. This is what has worked for me.

The more you can keep it personal, the more you can show them what it is that you needed to do, in order to achieve this, its all yours and they make the choice of if they want to check it out. When you have someone approaching you out of intrigue you have the upper hand as well. They came to you, they saw something in you they want. They have already signed up in their head, even if at this point they know not what.

You can give someone 100 samples of things. Its not until they have a reason to open the bottle, or package that it will it mean anything. Something can smell nice but until they see it in you, there is nothing for them, no incentive.

So, when I say drop the ego mania, I also am saying embrace it. Because its all about you. However, it is not all about changing them, it becomes all about you and the changes you have made. A business is a lifestyle. I am not talking about the ability to lounge on a boat all day long. That is a life choice. The lifestyle is really all about what you have learned, how it has changed you, and how it has showed you the ability to make different life choices.

So take a moment and write down all the things that your business has already brought to you. What things have you been able to manifest? What do you think that your product or service can bring to you. Work on those. We spend way to much time trying to figure out how to say things to people and not enough time thinking about what we are gonna say to them.

Chapter 5: Keeping Your Friends and Family.

As we mentioned in the previous chapter sometimes

we can become the next evangelical of marketing, and if our family or friends consistently hear about all of our services and products the thing that most of them will think about is why they don't make an anti-annoying cream.

Where I mentioned before its a friends job to listen where its a relationship where you can't. Well there is a limit too. There are three things that you have to make sure of when you are marketing to your close friends and family.

1. Use what they ask for, not what you want for them.

2. TAKE TIME

3. Family First Business second.

The first one I can be a hard one. We all want better for our friends and family, however most times that people are hearing about your business is when you are gathered with them, you "happen" to bring it up. Its not them saying: "Hey, wanna tell us how we need to spend money?"

Most business and network marketing have a bad name when you start them. Its the most business fail, or network marketing is just a way to make others money. This can raise many red flags, with people that are close to us will want to impart on you the knowledge of someone who has failed.

The best thing to do is when someone complains about, or makes mention to something that they need help with, you offer them the product. NOT the business. Most people could care less or do not think about having their own business. Or if you are in a service industry they don't wanna know what they need, they just want it to go away. Its about showing them that they can have both.

Take time. Do not expect people to fall right in line right away. They have seen you in your life probably pick up many things that were gonna change the world, or know others that are close to them, that do the same thing. What you need to do is just let people know slowly in the family, invite them to mixers, or open houses or celebrations. Know that you are still learning and this is what I think works.

This way you can let them come to you and not feeling pressured. Since they are around you have many times to advertise to them. Don't make them wanna change the channel on the infomercial. It can and will also make people feel insulted. Before you found this product were you so out of whack that you couldn't live? Probably not. When you say things like oh when you are ready to be healthy, or when you are ready to start getting better financially think about what you are actually saying to the friends and family.

People will not want to get your products or services when they feel like they are being lectured by the person providing the service or products. Guilt only works when your mother wants to make a point. Not when you are trying to be successful.

Family first. Most families are defective to the person in the middle of them. We all want people to do better, and when its family we want them to work and when we have found something that works we want to immediately again share the good news.

There is always something but family first. When the family is talking about debt, its not time to pull out the compensation plan. Its time to be apart of the family. This will foster. Intellectual maturity means knowing when to offer things to people at the appropriate time. When you don't have time to be a family or friend, it shows that your model is not working, and that you have to spend every second of what you are doing, working your business. That

REAKS of desperation and that you are not being honest about your success.

Take a look at your life. Schedule out time that you are gonna spend on your business and time you are going to spend elsewhere. Making sure that the elsewhere stuff is much bigger than the business. Yes you have to work the business but have times, and don't become the business. You have more aspects to you, and you have to honor each and every step.

www.ingramcontent.com/pod-product-compliance
Lightning Source LLC
Chambersburg PA
CBHW071827170526
45167CB00003B/1455